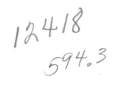
SNAILS

designed and written by Althea
illustrated by Helen Herbert

Longman Group USA Inc.

Published in the United States of America by Longman Group USA Inc.
© 1983, 1988 Althea Braithwaite

Originally published in Great Britain in a slightly altered form by Longman Group UK Limited

ISBN: 0-88462-192-8   (library bound)
ISBN: 0-88462-193-6   (paperback)

Printed in the United States of America

88 89 90 10 9 8 7 6 5 4 3 2 1

Library of Congress Cataloging-in-Publication Data

Althea.
  Snails / designed and written by Althea ; illustrated by Helen Herbert.
  p.   cm.--(Life-cycle books / Althea)
  Summary: Describes the appearance, habits, reproduction, and growth of this mollusk that lives in cool, wet, and shady places.
  1. Snails--Juvenile literature. [1. Snails] I. Herbert, Helen, ill. II. Title. III. Series: Althea.   Life-cycle books.
QL430.4.A63   1988
594'.3--dc19   88-8509
ISBN 0-88462-192-8   CIP
ISBN 0-88462-193-6 (pbk.)   AC

Notes for parents and teachers

Life-Cycle Books have been specially written and designed as a simple, yet informative, series of factual nature books for young children.

The illustrations are bright and clear, and children can "read" the pictures while the story is read to them.

The text has been specially set in large type to make it easy for children to follow along or even to read for themselves.

It is spring.
The snails come
out after their
long winter rest.
They live under
stones or leaves,
where it is cool,
wet and shady.

At night, two snails
glide around and
touch each other with
tentacles, which
are their feelers.
They mate, and eggs
grow in each snail.

Two weeks or so pass.
Each snail makes a hole
in the ground and
lays its eggs.
The eggs are covered
with soil to keep them safe.

A snail with its
own shell grows in
each egg.

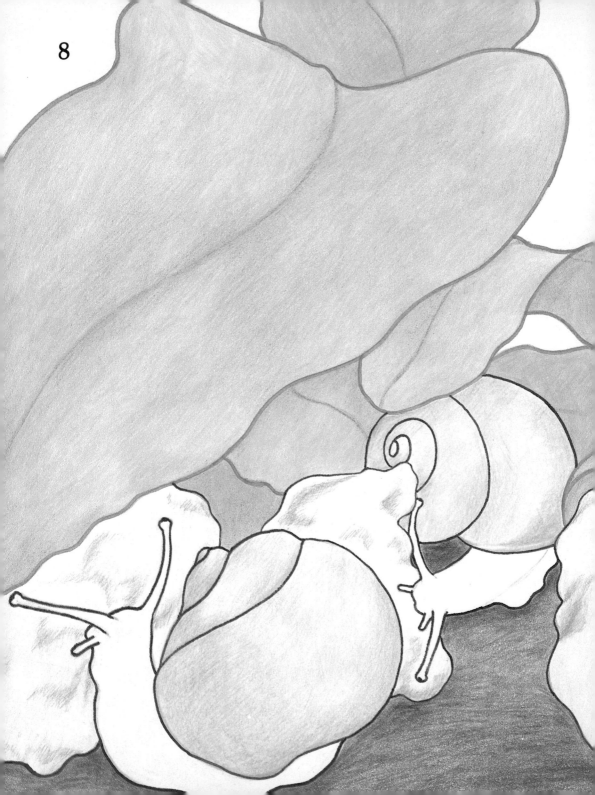

When the eggs hatch,
the tiny snails
eat their eggshells.

Each baby snail
eats grass and plants
and soon starts to grow.
Its shell grows too.

Every summer night
snails hunt for food.
Their long tongues are covered
with thousands of tiny teeth
to chew rotting leaves and plants.
Snails need food to grow and
to store in their bodies for winter.

A snail moves slowly
about on its foot.
The snail makes a slime
to help it slide along
without hurting itself.
Slime helps a snail climb
walls without falling off.
It leaves a silvery trail
behind.

A snail has an eye
at the end of each of
two long tentacles.
It can only see light
and dark.

It uses its four tentacles
to touch, feel and smell.
It breathes through
a hole in its side.

Snails return to their
homes each day to rest
and hide from enemies.

In hot, dry weather snails
pull themselves inside
their shells and seal
the entrance. They open it
when the rain comes.

Winter is here.
The snails find
safe hiding places.
They seal their shells
shut and rest.

When spring comes
perhaps one snail will
mate with another
and they will lay eggs.

SNAILS are interesting because they are so different from most of the animals children can observe. Snails, with slugs, are one class of mollusks, animals with soft bodies usually protected by shells. The snails pictured here are land snails and differ from sea snails in a number of ways.

A snail must protect itself from cold in winter and absence of water in summer. It pulls itself into its shell and closes the entrance with a calcium seal. Its body functions decrease and it rests until conditions are right for it to emerge and find food. The shell continues to grow for several years; a snail's age can be guessed roughly from the shell's number of whorls or turns. Eight whorls means about two years old.

Land snails each have male and female reproductive organs, but an exchange of sperm between two snails is necessary if eggs are to be fertilized and hatched. Eggs deposited in the fall hatch in spring, when moisture and food are available.

Snails have many enemies: birds, racoons and other small animals, even other snails—and humans who prize one kind as a food delicacy. Certain snails, especially in Africa, destroy crops because of their numbers and voracious appetites. On the other hand, the destruction of a habitat by new land uses may threaten a particular variety of snail with extinction.